D0939711

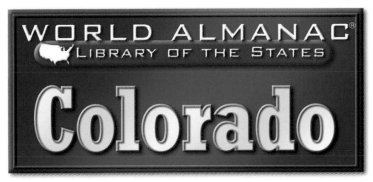

WORLD ALMANAC® LIBRARY OF THE STATES

Colorado

THE CENTENNIAL STATE

by Megan Elias

Curriculum Consultant: Jean Craven,
Director of Instructional Support,
Albuquerque, NM, Public Schools

WORLD ALMANAC® LIBRARY

Please visit our web site at: **www.worldalmanaclibrary.com**
For a free color catalog describing World Almanac® Library's
list of high-quality books and multimedia programs, call
1-800-848-2928 (USA) or 1-800-387-3178 (Canada).
World Almanac® Library's fax: (414) 332-3567.

Library of Congress Cataloging-in-Publication Data

Elias, Megan.
    Colorado, the Centennial State / by Megan Elias.
        p. cm. — (World Almanac Library of the states)
    Includes bibliographical references and index.
    Summary: Describes the history, people, geography, economy, government,
state events and attractions, and social life and customs of Colorado.
    ISBN 0-8368-5130-7 (lib. bdg.)
    ISBN 0-8368-5300-8 (softcover)
    1. Colorado—Juvenile literature. [1. Colorado.] I. Title. II. Series.
F776.3.E44   2002
978.8—dc21   2002023458

This edition first published in 2002 by
World Almanac® Library
330 West Olive Street, Suite 100
Milwaukee, WI 53212 USA

This edition © 2002 by World Almanac® Library.

Design and Editorial: Bill SMITH STUDIO Inc.
Editor: Anne Wright
Assistant Editor: Timothy Paulson
Art Director: Jay Jaffe
Photo Research: Sean Livingstone
World Almanac® Library Project Editor: Patricia Lantier
World Almanac® Library Editors: Monica Rausch, Catherine Gardner, Lyman Lyons,
 Jim Mezzanotte
World Almanac® Library Production: Tammy Gruenewald, Katherine A. Goedheer

Photo credits: pp. 4-5 © PhotoDisc; p. 6 (left) © Corel, (right) © PhotoDisc; p. 7 (top) © Dover,
(bottom) © Corel; p. 9 © PhotoDisc; p. 10 © Dover; p. 11 © Dover; p. 12 Denver Public Library;
p. 13 Denver Public Library; p. 14 Denver Public Library; p. 15 © Robert Holmes/CORBIS; p. 17
© Library of Congress; p. 18 © PhotoDisc; p. 19 © PhotoDisc; p. 20 (left to right) © PhotoDisc,
© PAINET INC., © Corel; p. 21 (left to right) © Corel, Boulder Convention & Visitors Bureau,
Denver Metro Convention & Visitors Bureau; p. 23 © PhotoDisc; p. 24 © PhotoDisc; p. 26 (top)
Denver Metro Convention & Visitors Bureau, (bottom) © PhotoDisc; p. 27 Denver Metro
Convention & Visitors Bureau; p. 29 Denver Metro Convention & Visitors Bureau; p. 31 © Library
of Congress; p. 32 © PhotoDisc; p. 33 Denver Metro Convention & Visitors Bureau; p. 34 Denver
Metro Convention & Visitors Bureau; p. 35 Denver Metro Convention & Visitors Bureau; p. 36 ©
Colin Braley/Reuters/TimePix; p. 37 © PhotoDisc; p. 38 © Dover; p. 39 © Dover; p. 40 (all)
© PhotoDisc; p. 41 © Time Magazine/TimePix; pp. 42-43 © Library of Congress; p. 44 (left)
© PhotoDisc, (right) © PhotoDisc; p. 45 (top) Denver Metro Convention & Visitors Bureau,
(bottom) © PhotoDisc

All rights reserved. No part of this book may be reproduced, stored in a retrieval system,
or transmitted in any form or by any means, electronic, mechanical, photocopying, recording,
or otherwise, without the prior written permission of the copyright holder.

Printed in the United States of America

1 2 3 4 5 6 7 8 9 06 05 04 03 02

Colorado

INTRODUCTION	4
ALMANAC	6
HISTORY	8
THE PEOPLE	16
THE LAND	20
ECONOMY & COMMERCE	24
POLITICS & GOVERNMENT	28
CULTURE & LIFESTYLE	32
NOTABLE PEOPLE	38
TIME LINE	42
STATE EVENTS & ATTRACTIONS	44
MORE ABOUT COLORADO	46
INDEX	47

A Striking State

Colorado is a state of breathtaking natural beauty and fascinating human history. The Rocky Mountains cut through the state and include the Continental Divide, which separates rivers that run east to the Atlantic Ocean and Gulf of Mexico, and west to the Pacific Ocean. Colorado rivers push their way through rock formations, creating deep canyons and revealing the remains of the massive creatures that inhabited the region long before humans arrived on the scene.

In the thirteenth century, an ancient people known as the Anasazi carved villages into the faces of the huge mesas, or flat-topped land formations, that distinguish the state's southwestern region. From their cliff dwellings, the Anasazi looked out on the splendor of what would one day be Colorado.

Pioneers did not come to the area in large numbers until gold was discovered near Denver in 1858. The chance to strike it rich seemed a glistening opportunity, and prospectors and settlers poured into the state in search of a golden, or at least a silver, future. In the 1870s, photographer William Henry Jackson traveled through the state, taking the striking pictures that would become the state's most enduring portrait.

Coloradans are willing to fight for their rights. In 1893, the spirited women of Colorado demonstrated for the right to vote and convinced the people of the state, who granted them full rights in a popular vote. In 1914, miners in Trinidad, Colorado, struck for fair treatment in what became known as the Ludlow Massacre. Through the years, Coloradans Barney Ford, Helen Hunt Jackson, and Benjamin Lindsey have defended the rights of minorities and children. Other famous people with ties to Colorado include musical pioneers such as Glenn Miller, remarkable athletes such as John Elway and Jack Dempsey, and groundbreaking scientists such as Florence Sabin. Today, Colorado is still a place where people are always willing to strike out in new directions.

▶ Map of Colorado showing the interstate highway system, as well as major cities and waterways.

▼ The twin peaks of the Maroon Bells rise over Maroon Lake. This spectacular scene is part of the Maroon Bells–Snowmass Wilderness, which includes more than 174,000 acres (70,418 hectares) in the White River and Gunnison National Forests.

COLORADO

WYOMING

NEBRASKA

Cheyenne

N

Little Snake R.

Yampa R.

White R.

Laramie R.

Colorado R.

Fort Collins

Grand Lake

L. Granby

Boulder

Golden

Denver

Lakewood

Aurora

Sterling

Greeley

South Platte R.

Arikaree R.

76

25

70

70

Vail

Leadville

Aspen

South Platte R.

Grand Junction

Gunnison R.

70

Burlington

KANSAS

Colorado Springs

Big Sandy Creek

UTAH

Montrose

Blue Mesa Res.

Canon City

Pueblo

Arkansas R.

Telluride

John Martin Res.

Dolores R.

Rio Grande

Durango

25

Ludlow

Purgatoire R.

Trinidad

ARIZONA

Farmington

NEW MEXICO

OK

SCALE/KEY

0   50 Miles

0   50 Kilometers

⭐ Capital

--- State Border

Interstate Highways

Fast Facts

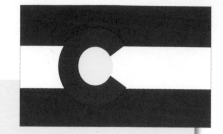

COLORADO (CO), The Centennial State

Entered Union

August 1, 1876 (38th state)

Capital	Population
Denver	554,636

Total Population (2000)

4,301,261 (24th most populous state) — *Between 1990 and 2000, the population of Colorado increased 30.6 percent.*

Largest Cities	Population
Denver	554,636
Colorado Springs	360,890
Aurora	276,393
Lakewood	144,126
Fort Collins	118,652

Land Area

103,718 square miles (268,630 square kilometers) (8th largest state)

State Motto

"Nil Sine Numine" — *Latin for* "Nothing Without the Deity"

State Song

"Where the Columbines Grow," *by A. J. Fynn, adopted in 1915*

State Animal

Rocky Mountain bighorn sheep — *Found only in the Rocky Mountains, this breed of wild sheep is noted for its agility. The male of the species has large horns that curve backward from the forehead.*

State Bird

Lark bunting

State Fish

Greenback cutthroat trout — *In the late 1980s, biologists feared that this colorful red-bellied, green-backed fish had been made extinct by pollution. Recently, however, several small populations of the fish have been discovered. The state plans to reintroduce it into more streams.*

State Insect

Colorado hairstreak butterfly

State Tree

Colorado blue spruce — *This tree, noted for its symmetrical triangular shape and its silver-blue color, was first discovered on Pikes Peak in 1862.*

State Flower

White and lavender columbine — *This delicate flower is rare. According to state law, it may be picked, but no one may gather more than twenty-five blossoms in a single day.*

State Gemstone

Aquamarine — *This gemstone, which ranges in hue from pale blue to deep bluish green, is found in the peaks of Mount Antero and White Mountain.*

State Fossil

Stegosaurus

PLACES TO VISIT

Bishop's Castle, *Beulah*

For more than thirty years, Jim Bishop has been building himself a castle out of stones and ornamental ironwork. The castle is still just a shell, but Bishop has no interest in stopping construction. When he is finished with his castle, he says, he will build one for his wife. The fantastic structure, with its recently added gold minarets, can be visited year-round.

Kit Carson County Carousel, *Burlington*

This is the oldest wooden carousel in the United States. It was built in 1905 and is still wearing its original coat of paint.

Red Rocks Park, *Morrison*

Located near Denver, the park is named for its towering sandstone rock formations. It includes a naturally formed outdoor amphitheater, which has hosted many musical and theatrical events.

For other places and events, see p. 44.

For other places and events, see p. 44.

BIGGEST, BEST, AND MOST

- The largest mesa in the world is Grand Mesa, located in Grand Mesa National Forest.
- Three-quarters of U.S. land 10,000 feet (3,048 meters) or more above sea level is in Colorado.

STATE FIRSTS

- **1921** The first opera to be broadcast in its entirety over the radio was *Martha*, broadcast from Denver.
- **1934** The first train to travel 1,000 miles (1,609 km) without stopping left Union Station in Denver with eighty-five passengers and crew and arrived at the Halstead Street station in Chicago thirteen hours and five minutes later. The train, named the *Zephyr*, traveled 1,015 miles (1,633 km) at an average speed of 77.6 miles (125 km) per hour.

Colorado the Beautiful

In 1893, Katherine Lee Bates of Falmouth, Massachusetts, climbed to the top of Pikes Peak. She was so moved by the scenery stretched out below her that she wrote a poem about what she saw. The poem, "America the Beautiful," was published in *The Congregationalist* magazine in 1895. It was later set to the tune "Materna" by Samuel Ward and became an unofficial national anthem. Singer Ray Charles recorded a hit version in the 1970s. The song won new popularity after the terrorist attack of September 11, 2001, when people preferred to celebrate the nation's beauty rather than sing about "bombs bursting in air."

From Colorado with Love

Since 1947, millions of people have sent their Valentine's Day cards to be postmarked in Colorado. These people want to get the town of Loveland's special postmark to give their valentines extra sweetness. In 1946, Ted Thompson, then head of the town's chamber of commerce, and his wife Mabel came up with the idea and  put it into practice the next year. The Loveland post office receives hundreds of thousands of valentines each year. In addition to the romantic postmark, each valentine is stamped with a four-line valentine from the town, ensuring that each recipient gets a double dose of love.

Great Prospects

Westward! Ho! It is the sixteenth of the second month A.D. 1830 and I have joined a trapping, trading, hunting expedition to the Rocky Mountains. Why, I scarcely know, for the motives that induced me to this step were of a mixed complexion.

— *Warren Angus Ferris,* Life in The Rocky Mountains, 1830–1835

Archaeologists have found evidence that humans lived in the area we know as Colorado as early as twelve thousand years ago. Little is known about their way of life, however. More is known about the Anasazi, a people who inhabited the area as early as 1500 B.C. The Anasazi are now known for the distinctive baskets they wove, as well as for the villages that they built into the sides of mesas. Today, these villages are known as pueblos, from the Spanish word for town or village.

For a period of about one hundred years, the Anasazi lived in the pueblos they built high in cliff walls. Archaeologists and historians refer to the Anasazi of this period as the Cliff Dwellers. For a variety of reasons, possibly including changes in climate and depletion of natural resources, the Anasazi abandoned their cliff houses between A.D 1276 and 1300. The Ute Indians are thought to have settled in the area around A.D. 1500. Other Native American peoples, such as the Arapaho, Cheyenne, and Comanche, also lived in the region.

Native Americans of Colorado
Arapaho
Cheyenne
Comanche
Pueblo
Ute

European Exploration

In 1682, French explorer René-Robert Cavelier, Sieur de La Salle, claimed all the land drained by the Mississippi River for France. He had been given authority to do so by Louis XIV, king of France, and he named the area Louisiana. La Salle never actually saw Colorado, and he did not negotiate treaties with the peoples living in any of the regions he claimed.

The first Europeans — Spanish explorers — arrived in Colorado in the 1700s. Before the Spanish arrived, however, Native Americans in the area had already become acquainted with aspects of Spanish culture. The Ute, who had moved to the Colorado region from Utah, had traded elk and deer hides for Spanish horses and metal goods in the Rio Grande Valley.

Among the early Europeans was a band of Spanish soldiers who entered the territory in 1706 under the command of Juan de Ulibarri. He claimed the area for Spain. Spanish explorers were looking for gold. When they did not find it, they left without establishing settlements.

The Movement West

In 1803, eastern Colorado was included in one of history's most famous land deals, the Louisiana Purchase. United States president Thomas Jefferson bought the land La Salle had claimed for France in 1682. The total purchase price was $15 million — about 3 cents per acre (7 cents per ha). Two U.S. explorers later visited the area: Zebulon Pike came in 1806, and Stephen Long led an expedition through the region in 1820. After Long, hardy fur trappers known as mountain men began establishing trading posts. They traded furs and goods with the Native Americans.

The southern and western part of the region remained under Spanish control and became the property of Mexico

DID YOU KNOW?

Colorado takes its name from the Colorado River, which was named in 1706 by a party of Spanish explorers led by Juan de Ulibarri. The river was so named because mineral deposits in the riverbed made the water appear red. *Colorado* is Spanish for "red-colored."

▼ The Cliff Palace in Mesa Verde National Park was once a village that included two hundred rooms. The Anasazi, who lived there, plastered the interior walls of some rooms and also painted pictures on them.

when Mexico gained its independence from Spain in 1821. The Mexican government offered plots of land to anyone who would settle the area along its northern border, but few people accepted this offer. In 1848, at the end of the Mexican War, the United States took over the area that would form the southern part of Colorado. The first permanent U.S. settlement in Colorado was founded in 1851 at San Luis.

The Gold Rush, Farming, and the Civil War

In 1858, William Russell found gold at the point where Cherry Creek and the South Platte River meet. This sparked a gold rush similar to the one that had drawn thousands of people to California in 1849. Approximately fifty thousand people in search of gold moved to Colorado between 1858 and 1859. A group of men from the Kansas Territory settled on Cherry Creek and named their new town Denver, after James Denver, then the governor of the Kansas Territory. The settlement grew into the state's wealthiest and most important city.

Many miners left Colorado when the gold rush failed to bring them instant riches, but some remained to farm. Farms and ranches began to encroach on land where Native Americans had traditionally hunted, and hostilities grew between settlers and Native Americans.

DID YOU KNOW?

Victor was one of Colorado's gold rush towns. To commemorate its role in state history, the town's streets are paved with low-quality gold.

▼ Denver as it looked in the summer of 1859, when the Pikes Peak gold rush was under way. By the early years of the twentieth century, as much as $100 million in gold had been mined in the region.

In February 1861, the U.S. government created the Colorado Territory out of portions of four preexisting territories: Kansas, Nebraska, New Mexico, and Utah. Two months later, the Civil War began. Most of the federal troops posted in Colorado to protect the claims of settlers against raids by Native Americans were withdrawn to fight in the east.

Coloradans then raised volunteer militia units to fight alongside the Union Army. John Chivington, a Methodist minister, led one of these units. After successfully battling Confederate soldiers in New Mexico, Chivington and his band returned to Colorado, where tensions between settlers and Native Americans were escalating.

In retaliation for attacks by Cheyenne and Arapaho against settlers, the 3rd Colorado Cavalry, led by Chivington, attacked a Native American camp on November 29, 1864. The attack came at dawn, so most of the Native Americans were still asleep. Several hundred men, women, and children were killed in what became known as the Sand Creek Massacre. The event raised national awareness about the plight of Native Americans.

Despite this new concern, the U.S. Army entered Colorado in 1867 and forced almost all of the Native Americans onto reservations in Oklahoma. The Southern Ute, who lived on the plains, were among the few groups allowed to remain.

Statehood and Beyond

Colorado Territory settlers first asked for statehood in 1864, but, in part because the population was small, the request was not granted until 1876. Because Colorado became a state during the nation's centennial, or one hundredth anniversary of the signing of the Declaration of Independence, it earned the nickname "the Centennial State."

Going West

In the 1850s, Horace Greeley, an influential newspaper publisher in New York City, urged young men to leave the East Coast. Greeley thought that there were more opportunities for young people in the West than in the more densely populated and developed eastern part of the country. Greeley did not stop at encouraging migration, however. He also sponsored Union Colony, a utopian community in Colorado. A utopian community is one in which daily life is planned before people arrive in an attempt to create a perfect society. Union Colony was established in 1870 by Nathan C. Meeker, who was the agricultural editor of Greeley's newspaper, the *New York Tribune*, and a small group of settlers. They had agreed to practice agriculture, irrigation, and cooperation, to abstain from alcohol, and to support education and religion. The community, later named Greeley, flourished, opening a school in 1872 and a college in 1889. Meeker became a government representative to the Ute reservation and was killed in a violent uprising in 1879.

Between 1870 and 1890, the population of Colorado increased more than 1,000 percent, from about 40,000 to 412,000. The increase was primarily due to the growth of ranching and the rise of silver mining after the metal was discovered in Georgetown in 1864. The vast plains offered grazing land for the livestock of wealthy men who became known as cattle barons. The men who made their fortune from silver mining were known as silver kings or carbonate kings, named for the deposits of lead carbonate where silver was found. Most Coloradans were not barons or kings. They practiced farming or ranching in the eastern plains of the state. Farmers and ranchers were often at odds over the issues of fencing and water rights. These differences sometimes led to hostilities known as range wars.

Range wars often became violent. Cattle ranchers cut down fences so their cattle could graze freely and slaughtered flocks of sheep because sheep competed with cows for grazing land. Meanwhile, rustlers stole cattle to add to their own ranches. Farmers, angered by cattle trampling through and eating their crops, sometimes killed these four-footed trespassers. Animals were not the only casualties. The violence also resulted in deaths in both the farming and the ranching communities.

Non-Native settlement in western Colorado in the 1870s angered the Ute. In 1879, after having been forced onto a reservation, a band of Ute rebelled. The Ute killed Nathan Meeker, who was the federal representative to the reservation, and his staff. The Ute then were forced to

DID YOU KNOW?

Among those who rushed to Colorado in the mid-1800s was a legendary female miner, Caroline Mallen. Not much is known about her life. She was born in 1829 either in Ohio or Michigan and moved west sometime later. In Colorado, she earned fame for prospecting a number of very successful mines on Mount Elbert. Other miners noted her great skill in blasting, drilling, and hauling, as well as her ability to sew a silk dress. She seems to have been a believer in Spiritualism, a nineteenth-century religious movement, and she claimed that spirits told her where to dig.

▼ This nineteenth-century farm is now the site of Wheat Ridge, a Denver suburb.

disband, and many were expelled from the state.

Silver Blues

Although silver mining made a few people very wealthy, the industry struggled throughout the 1870s and 1880s because the U.S. government had stopped coining silver dollars. The

▲ Ludlow mine workers, who went on strike in 1913, moved into a tent colony set up by their union, the United Mine Workers of America.

1890 Sherman Silver Purchase Act had allowed some silver dollars to be minted, but it was repealed in 1893. Silver mines across Colorado closed. An attempt to get the federal government to mint silver coins again became a major issue for the Populist party.

Democratic presidential candidate William Jennings Bryan made his famous "Cross of Gold" speech in 1896, urging a return to silver money in the United States. Bryan said that using a gold, rather than a silver, standard would ruin the U.S. economy. Bryan lost his bid for the presidency to William McKinley.

Government policies were not the only troubles mine owners faced. Brutal labor conditions led to dissatisfaction among mine workers. Strikes were common — and violent. In 1880, miners in Leadville walked off the job, in part because their employer had forbidden them to talk while they were working. The employer responded by calling in a hired army and forcing the strikers out of the area.

The most tragic strike-related event began in 1913 in Ludlow, where coal miners worked for a company owned by John D. Rockefeller, one of the world's richest men. Rockefeller owned the mine and the town where the workers lived. When the workers went on strike for better pay and working conditions, Rockefeller evicted them from their houses. Twelve hundred strikers settled in a tent village outside of town. National Guard troops were sent in to control confrontations between strikers and company-hired guards. On April 20, 1914, violence escalated into a day-long battle. Among those killed were about a dozen women and children. Violence spread to other mining areas until federal troops were sent in.

Helping Hand

In 1859, Clara Brown, a former slave from Virginia, moved to Colorado. Brown is thought to be the first African-American woman to enter the state. She set up a laundry in Central City, a mining community, and made enough money to invest in land. Women who provided domestic services such as laundry or cooking could often make quite a lot of money in the mostly male-populated towns. In 1866, having saved about $10,000, Brown began trying to find her family, from whom she'd been separated as a slave. In the process, she helped many former slaves move to Colorado.

A New Golden Age

In the 1890s, Colorado's mining industry took an upturn after Robert Womack discovered gold at Cripple Creek. For many years thereafter, Colorado was one of the most productive gold-mining regions in the world. The city of Denver flourished during the 1890s. The state's strong independent streak showed itself as women gained the right to vote in all state elections in 1893. It was the second state to give women the vote, but the first to make the decision through a popular election.

▲ Oil drilling rigs began extracting underground oil in Colorado in the 1860s and reached peak production in the 1920s, when this photograph was taken.

In 1914, as World War I began, new markets opened up for U.S. metals and food products. Colorado's economy became healthier as the state helped to satisfy the growing demand for food and natural resources. The state experienced an economic boom, as mining expanded to tungsten and molybdenum, two metallic elements used in steel processing. Oil, which had first been discovered in Colorado in the 1860s, became an increasingly important product and contributed to the boom. In the 1920s, Colorado oil wells in places such as Craig and Fort Collins, where oil was discovered in 1923, produced nearly five million barrels a year.

Hard Times and Recovery

The Great Depression, which began with the stock market crash of 1929, brought hard times to Colorado. A drought that lasted from 1932 to 1937 added to the misery of the times. Banks failed and farmers were forced to abandon their land. Silver and gold mining were not affected by the Depression, however, and production actually increased throughout the 1930s. This was partly the result of the Legal Tender Act of 1933 and the Gold Reserve Act of 1934. Both were part of President Franklin Roosevelt's New Deal, a collection of programs designed to help the nation recover from the Depression.

In 1934, the U.S. government passed the Reorganization Act, which helped Colorado's Native American peoples to

DID YOU KNOW?

In 1905, Colorado had three governors in one day. After an election marred by accusations of voting fraud by both parties, Democrat Alva Adams took office. Republicans, however, insisted that the count had not been accurate and replaced him with incumbent governor James Peabody. Democrats objected to this so strenuously that the legislature decided neither man should be governor. Instead, they promoted Jesse McDonald, the lieutenant governor, to the office.

reacquire land that was confiscated from them in the 1800s. In 1936, the Southern Ute tribe approved the constitution and laws that now govern the group. The Ute Mountain Ute tribe adopted its constitution in 1940.

During and after World War II, manufacturing became increasingly important in Colorado and helped to boost the state's economy. Wartime defense plants and military training camps were established in the state. The advent of the atomic age made uranium mining big business for about forty years after the war.

After the war, tourism became an important component of the Colorado economy. New interstate highways brought vacationers to enjoy the scenery. The growth of skiing as a popular leisure activity made small mountain towns, such as Vail and Aspen, into popular ski resorts.

From the 1950s into the 21st century, the population has been shifting westward into the center of the state. Farming, mostly centered in the east, has become unprofitable on a small scale, and people have left rural areas for service and manufacturing jobs in the cities.

Today, as the population shifts into more concentrated areas, environmental issues are coming to the forefront of state politics. While 90 percent of the population lives east of the Continental Divide, the majority of the water is in the west. Projects to reroute water into the more populated parts of the state have angered both farmers in the west and environmentalists.

Technology industries, such as those involving communications and computers, experienced an enormous growth spurt in the 1990s in Colorado, particularly around Denver. This economic growth helped the state draw two new major sports franchises to the Denver area. Major League Baseball's Colorado Rockies came first, in 1993, followed by the Quebec Nordique in 1995 (they became the Colorado Avalanche).

Slalom for Uncle Sam

During World War II, battles took place in Europe's mountains. U.S. troops, however, had not been trained for this kind of combat. Charles Dole, the chairman of the National Ski Patrol, approached President Franklin Roosevelt and offered to train soldiers in skiing and mountaineering skills. Eventually, a training base was set up at Camp Hale, in Colorado, and there skier-soldiers formed the 10th Mountain Division. When they returned home after the war, several division members established ski schools in Colorado and other mountain states, contributing to the postwar interest in recreational skiing. Vail (*pictured below*) and Aspen are among the resorts started by former members of the 10th Mountain Division.

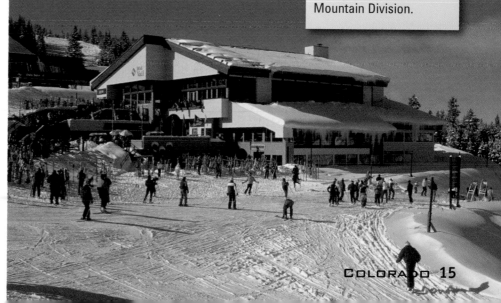

Above It All

> You know I love the trail I'm on
> And the friends who ride with me
> The country that we're passing through
> Is a paradise to see.
>
> — *from "Durango Mountain Caballero",*
> *song by John Denver*

A round 1910, Colorado's population shifted from primarily rural to mostly urban. As manufacturing replaced agriculture as the state's main industry, people moved to urban areas to work in factories and service-sector jobs. Today, about 80 percent of all Coloradans live in cities such as Denver and Colorado Springs. Most of Colorado's major cities are located in a small area of the state on the eastern edge of the Rocky Mountains. The mountains themselves are sparsely populated.

A Varied Tapestry

Of all the groups that have settled in Colorado, the Ute have been there the longest. Small family groups once traveled together throughout the region during the warmer months

Age Distribution in Colorado
(2000 Census)

0–4	297,505
5–19	927,163
20–24	306,238
25–44	1,400,850
45–64	953,432
65 & over	416,073

Across One Hundred Years

Colorado's three largest foreign-born groups for 1890 and 1990

1890			1990		
Germany	England	Ireland	Mexico	Germany	Canada
15,151	14,406	12,352	34,261	14,466	8,789

Total state population: 412,198
Total foreign-born: 83,990 (20%)

Total state population: 3,294,394
Total foreign-born: 142,434 (4%)

Patterns of Immigration

The total number of people who immigrated to Colorado in 1998 was 6,513. Of that number, the largest immigrant groups were from Mexico (35.2%), China (4.9%), and Vietnam (4.4%).

as they hunted game and gathered plants and berries for food. In the winter, larger groups gathered to spend the cold months together. The Ute now live mostly on two reservations in the southwestern corner of the state, the Southern Ute reservation in Ignacio and the Ute Mountain reservation in Towaoc. Today, approximately forty-four thousand Native Americans from various tribal groups live in the state.

The great majority of Colorado's population — more than 80 percent — is of northern European descent. Among the first non-Native settlers to arrive in the region were men and women from Cornwall, England, where there were many tin mines. These immigrants brought their mining skills and settled in mining communities. Among Colorado's other settlers in the nineteenth century were immigrants from central Europe who established farms in the eastern part of the state.

▲ The Ute camp at the Garden of the Gods in 1913.

Heritage and Background, Colorado — Year 2000

▶ Here's a look at the racial backgrounds of Coloradans today. Colorado ranks thirty-second among all U.S. states with regard to African Americans as a percentage of the population.

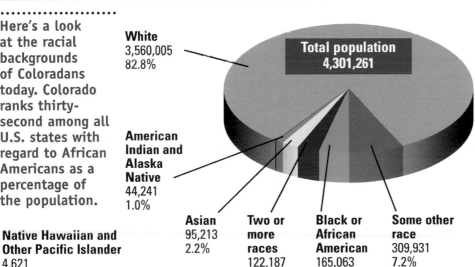

White
3,560,005
82.8%

Total population
4,301,261

American Indian and Alaska Native
44,241
1.0%

Native Hawaiian and Other Pacific Islander
4,621
0.1%

Asian
95,213
2.2%

Two or more races
122,187
2.8%

Black or African American
165,063
3.8%

Some other race
309,931
7.2%

Note: 17.1% (735,601) of the population identify themselves as **Hispanic** or **Latino,** a cultural designation that crosses racial lines. Hispanics and Latinos are counted in this category as well as the racial category of their choice.

The state's history as part of the Spanish colonial empire and as a possession of Mexico is reflected in its significant Hispanic population — 17 percent.

African Americans began to arrive in Colorado in the 1850s. One of the first people to discover gold in the state was Henry Parker, an African-American man who owned a mine in Idaho Springs. Historians estimate that about one-third of the cowboys who worked on ranches in the West were African American. The Asian population of Colorado is about 2 percent and includes immigrants and descendants of recent immigrants from China, Vietnam, and the Philippines.

Colorado Today

Coloradans are never out of sight of breathtaking natural scenery. Thousands of acres of public land are maintained in the state. Colorado's population includes the largest

Queen of the Plains

Denver has been rated one of the top ten financial centers in the world. It also offers recreational opportunities. The City and County of Denver, which are one unit, have a total of thirty-one named public parks and sixteen unnamed plots of parkland, comprising about 14,000 acres (5,666 ha) of land set aside for public enjoyment.

Educational Levels of Colorado Workers (age 25 and over)	
Less than 9th grade	118,252
9th to 12th grade, no diploma	209,804
High school graduate, including equivalency	558,312
Some college, no degree or associate degree	652,448
Bachelor's degree	379,150
Graduate or professional degree	189,106

▼ Snowcapped mountains tower over the skyline of Denver, Colorado's most populous city.

number of college graduates in the United States. Coloradans have a high standard of living. In 1999, the per capita personal income in the state was $31,533, well above the national figure of $28,546. In the same year, the unemployment rate in the state was a low 2.9 percent.

Denver is Colorado's largest city. It is known as the Mile High City because of its elevation, and as the Queen City of the Plains because it was the first major metropolis in the state. Twenty-five miles (40 km) northwest of Denver, Boulder is surrounded by 30,000 acres (12,140 ha) of open space. The University of Colorado has a campus in Boulder with approximately twenty-five thousand students.

▲ Junior high school students attend a computer lab in Golden.

Religion

More than three-quarters of Coloradans identify themselves as Christians. The largest single group of Christians is the 22 percent who are Catholic. Protestant denominations are also represented. About 10 percent of the population are Baptist, 7.7 percent are Methodist, and others are Lutheran, Episcopalian, and Evangelical. Among the state's non-Christians are the 1.4 percent who are Jewish, the 0.2 percent who are Hindu, the 0.1 percent who are Buddhist, and the ten thousand Coloradans who practice Islam. One percent of the population identify themselves as agnostic, neither believing nor disbelieving in God.

Education

The first school in Colorado opened in 1859 in Auraria, a gold-rush town that is now part of Denver. Its students were children of miners. In 1861, when Colorado became a territory, free public schools were established. Colorado is home to twenty-nine public and twenty-nine private four-year institutions of higher learning, including the University of Colorado, which has four campuses, and the Air Force Academy in Colorado Springs, which opened in 1958.

National Tragedy

In April 1999, national attention was tragically drawn to Littleton, a Denver suburb, when two teenaged boys opened fire on their classmates at Columbine High School. The two teens killed twelve students and a teacher and wounded twenty-three others before killing themselves. The event sparked national debates about the availability of guns and the violent nature of some video games and movies.

Purple Mountains Majesty

> Immediately overhead Pikes Peak, at an elevation of 12,000 feet above the level of the sea, towers high into the clouds; whilst from the fountain, like a granitic amphitheatre, ridge after ridge, clothed with pine and cedar, rises and meets the stupendous mass of mountains.
>
> — *George Frederick Ruxton*, Wild Life in the Rocky Mountains, *1916*

From the rugged Rocky Mountains to the windblown Great Plains, Colorado is a land of variety. It is the highest state in the nation. The average elevation of the state is 6,800 feet (2,073 m) above sea level. The state's lowest point is on the Arikaree River in northeastern Colorado, at 3,315 feet (1,010 m) above sea level. The terrain rises to 14,433 feet (4,399 m) above sea level at the peak of Mount Elbert. Along the peaks of the Rockies runs the Continental Divide, which separates the rivers that drain west to the Pacific Ocean from those that drain east to the Atlantic Ocean and Gulf of Mexico.

Colorado is an almost perfect rectangle. Its straight borders run about 380 miles (611 km) east to west and almost 280 miles (450 km) north to south. In the southwest, Colorado's borders form a junction with those of Utah, Arizona, and New Mexico, creating an area known as the Four Corners region. The state's terrain can be divided into three major areas: the Rocky Mountains, the Great Plains, and the Colorado Plateau.

Highest Point
Mount Elbert
14,433 feet (4,399 m) above sea level

▼ *From left to right:* a shining Amtrak train passes through the countryside near Durango; Mt. Elbert; aspen and pine trees thrive in the Colorado Rockies; a bull moose in the wild; an aerial view of Boulder; Echo Lake.

The Mountains

The Rockies are Colorado's most dramatic physical feature. They form a strip 75 to 100 miles (120 to 161 km) wide that runs north-south through the middle of the state. Within Colorado's portion of the Rockies can be found the towering Pikes Peak, at 14,110 feet (4,301 m), and Mount Elbert, the highest peak in the entire Rocky Mountain range, at 14,433 feet (4,399 m). The Colorado Rockies can be divided into roughly five ranges: the Front Range in the east and the Sangre de Cristo Mountains to their south; the Park Range in the west; the Sawatch Range, lying south of the Park Range; and the San Juan Mountains in southwestern Colorado.

Plateaus and Plains

On the western side of the Rocky Mountains, the Colorado Plateau covers about one-fifth of the state's land area. Farmers grow crops in its valleys, while ranchers graze sheep on grasses at the tops of its mesas. East of the Rockies, the Great Plains stretch over about two-fifths of the state. These plains have been irrigated in the twentieth century to make large-scale agriculture possible.

Lakes and Rivers

During the most recent ice age, glaciers made deep cuts in the Rocky Mountains. As the glaciers melted, the water filled the depressions, creating lakes high in the mountains. Grand Lake, Colorado's largest natural lake, covers about 600 acres (243 ha) and is 250 feet (76 m) deep at its deepest point. Larger, artificially-created lakes include Lake Granby, which covers 7,260 acres (2,938 ha).

Many rivers flow through Colorado, in some places cutting deep gorges in the rock and in others tumbling over rocks to create beautiful waterfalls. The highest suspension bridge in the United States stretches across

Average January temperature
Durango: 22°F (-6°C)
Fort Collins: 28°F (-2°C)

Average July temperature
Durango: 69°F (21°C)
Fort Collins: 72°F (22°C)

Average yearly rainfall
Durango: 18 inches (46 cm)
Fort Collins: 14.4 inches (37 cm)

Average yearly snowfall
Durango: 63 inches (160 cm)
Fort Collins: 50.9 inches (129 cm)

Major Rivers

Rio Grande	1,900 miles (3,057 km)
Arkansas River	1,459 miles (2,348 km)
Colorado River	1,450 miles (2,333 km)
South Platte River	424 miles (682 km)

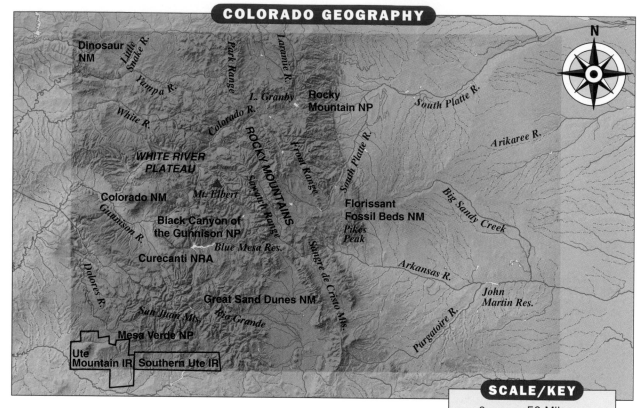

the Arkansas River's Royal Gorge. The river lies
1,053 feet (321 m) below.

Plants and Animals

Nearly one-third of Colorado is covered in forests.
The Colorado blue spruce, the state tree, grows in the
higher mountain areas. Only grasses and scrub plants
grow among the rocks above the timberline, which
starts at approximately 11,500 feet (3,505 m). Some
mountaintops have year-round snowcaps. Ponderosa
pines, important to Colorado's lumber industry, grow
on the Rockies' lower slopes. Trees that grow at lower
altitudes include aspens, cottonwoods, and maples.
Before being settled, the Great Plains were covered
in wild grasses. Now these grasses are mostly limited
to uncultivated areas. In particularly dry parts of the
plains, desert plants such as cactus and yucca can be found.

Colorado wildflowers appear in the high mountains as
soon as the snow melts. Buttercups, sky pilots, and old
man of the mountains bloom in high altitudes, while
lilies and larkspurs provide color on the plains.

SCALE/KEY

0	50 Miles
0	50 Kilometers

IR	Indian Reservation
NP	National Park
NRA	National Recreation Area
NM	National Monument
▲	Highest Point
	Mountains

DID YOU KNOW?

The lowest point in Colorado is higher than the highest point in Pennsylvania.

Among the animals that live in the mountains are bears, bighorn sheep, moose, foxes, and porcupines. After having been hunted and driven from their habitats, mountain lions are making a comeback. Prairie dogs, ground squirrels, coyotes, and western rattlesnakes populate the plains. Golden eagles make their nests, called aeries, in the rocks of the high mountains.

Colorado's lakes and rivers are home to kokanee salmon, bass, and several kinds of trout, which are popular with anglers. Coloradans have set limits on the number of fish that may be caught, as well as the number of game animals, such as deer and duck, that can be hunted. The state breeds fish and restocks rivers and lakes to maintain populations.

Climate

Weather in Colorado is generally dry and sunny, although average temperatures vary widely. On the plains, the summers are hot and dry, while in the mountains they are cool and dry. Most places cool down significantly at night. The state's average yearly precipitation, which includes both snow and rain, is 15 inches (38 centimeters), but this is not distributed evenly across the state. More precipitation falls on the western slopes of the Rockies than on the plains.

Divine Gift

In 1909, the children of Charles Perkins, who made his fortune in railroads, gave a present to the city of Colorado Springs. Honoring their father's wishes, they donated 480 acres (194 ha) of the "Garden of the Gods" to the city. The Garden of the Gods is an area of magnificent red sandstone rock formations. European Americans first saw and named the site in 1859, but archaeologists have evidence that people lived in the area as far back as three thousand years ago.

Striking It Rich

> The men of the Rocky Mountain regions are impressed with the fact that they must not depend upon the East. . . . They believe . . . in the principle of self-maintenance; and acting thereupon, already the whir of the spindles, the blast of the forge, and the blow of the blacksmith's hammer are heard.
>
> — *"Colorado Manufacturers" in* The Manufacturer and Builder *magazine, 1869*

The Colorado economy varies from region to region across the state. Most farming and ranching takes place in the east, although sheep also are raised in the west. Central Colorado is home to major manufacturing interests, while mining is a significant industry on the western slopes of the Rocky Mountains. Tourism is big business throughout the state, especially in the Rocky Mountains, where resorts draw thousands of visitors throughout the year.

Farming and Ranching

Of the state's nearly 32 million acres (13 million ha) of agricultural land, only one-third is used to grow crops, which include wheat and hay. The rest serves as grazing land for cattle and sheep. Colorado is the fourth-largest producer of beef cattle in the United States. Most cattle ranching is found in the east, while sheep, grown for both wool and meat, graze on the tops of mesas in the western part of the state.

◄ A Colorado rancher rounds up his cattle.

Top Employers
(of workers age sixteen and over)

Services	34.9%
Wholesale and retail trade	21.9%
Manufacturing	12.7%
Transportation, communications, and other public utilities	8.2%
Finance, insurance, and real estate	7.3%
Construction	5.8%
Public Administration	5.1%
Agriculture, forestry, and fisheries	2.8%
Mining	1.3%

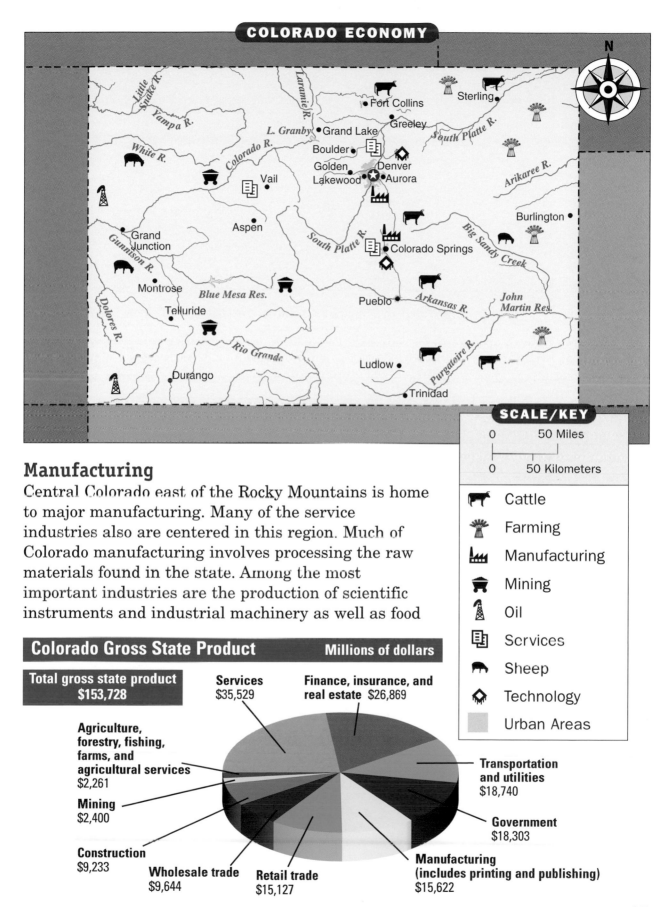

SCALE/KEY

0	50 Miles
0	50 Kilometers

Cattle
Farming
Manufacturing
Mining
Oil
Services
Sheep
Technology
Urban Areas

Manufacturing

Central Colorado east of the Rocky Mountains is home to major manufacturing. Many of the service industries also are centered in this region. Much of Colorado manufacturing involves processing the raw materials found in the state. Among the most important industries are the production of scientific instruments and industrial machinery as well as food

Colorado Gross State Product — Millions of dollars

Total gross state product $153,728

Services $35,529

Finance, insurance, and real estate $26,869

Agriculture, forestry, fishing, farms, and agricultural services $2,261

Mining $2,400

Construction $9,233

Wholesale trade $9,644

Retail trade $15,127

Manufacturing (includes printing and publishing) $15,622

Government $18,303

Transportation and utilities $18,740

processing. Colorado industries also produce parts for both guided missiles and vehicles used in outer space.

Denver is the state's center for food processing and beer brewing, which are the region's largest employers. The Coors Brewing Company has its headquarters in Golden, near Denver. The company helped fund the construction of Coors Field in Denver, home to Major League Baseball's Colorado Rockies.

▲ Coors Field is home to the Colorado Rockies. In recent years, a substantial amount of revenue has been generated by Denver's four major-league sports facilities.

Mining

In the mountains and on their western slopes, the main industries are mining and mineral extraction. Many of central Colorado's manufacturing plants are powered by coal mined in the west. Throughout the state, more than 7,000 oil wells produce 50,000 barrels of crude oil each day. Crude oil is refined to make gasoline and other petroleum products. The production of fossil fuels (coal, oil, and natural gas) makes up the great majority of the state's mineral output. Beneath the surface in western Colorado are huge deposits of shale oil, which can be used to produce crude oil. Efforts to extract the several billion barrels of oil, however, have not proved cost-effective. Colorado also ranks as the second-biggest U.S. producer of molybdenum, a metal that is used to strengthen steel.

◀ Colorado coal mining hit an all-time high of nearly 20 million tons in 1981.

Made in Colorado

Leading farm products and crops
Beef and other meats
Wheat
Feed grains
Vegetables

Other products
Electrical and non-electrical machinery
Processed and packaged foods
Telecommunications
Pharmaceuticals
Textiles

Transportation and Tourism

The Rocky Mountains have been a longtime barrier to transportation and commerce. In 1927, the Moffat Tunnel was completed 50 miles (80 km) west of Denver. This tunnel made transcontinental rail travel through the state possible for the first time. This 6-mile (10-km) tunnel shortened the railroad journey from Denver to the Pacific states by 176 miles (283 km).

Denver is Colorado's transportation hub. This role was staked out by the construction of the Moffat Tunnel and cemented by other projects in the twentieth century. In 1973, the Eisenhower Memorial Tunnel, constructed 60 miles (97 km) west of Denver, allowed cars and trucks to travel through the Rockies by going through the Continental Divide. Today, the tunnel carries traffic traveling west, and the Edwin C. Johnson Memorial Tunnel, built in 1979, serves traffic traveling east. While Colorado has seventeen commercial airports, Denver International Airport is its air hub. Colorado's transportation networks have allowed goods to flow more easily to and from the state. They have also made the state's natural beauty more accessible to people who live elsewhere. Tourists who visit Colorado to ski, hike, and enjoy the natural scenery spend about $8 billion a year in the state.

▼ Denver International Airport is among the busiest airports in the world. It also is rated as one of the most efficient airports in the United States.

Major Airports		
Airport	**Location**	**Passengers per year (2000)**
Denver International	Denver	38,751,687
Colorado Springs	Colorado Springs	2,424,701

United Across the Great Divide

Politics, like theater, is one of those things where you've got to be wise enough to know when to leave.

— *Richard Lamm, governor of Colorado, 1987, on stepping down after twelve years in office*

Since 1876, when it became a state, Colorado has had only one constitution. This constitution, however, may be amended, or changed. An amendment only becomes part of the constitution if a majority of voters approve it in an election. Amendments can be proposed by the legislature, by constitutional convention, or by initiative. In an initiative, a group of citizens proposes a change and collects enough signatures to indicate that the issue is important to a large number of people in the state. The number of signatures must equal 5 percent of the number of votes cast in the most recent election for secretary of state. In 2002, an initiative required 84,130 signatures. If the required signatures are obtained, the proposal will be placed on the ballot in a general election. Recent initiatives have involved term limits, campaign finance, taxes on tobacco, and bear hunting. As with the federal government, Colorado's state government is divided among the executive, legislative, and judicial branches.

Executive Branch

The executive branch of the Colorado state government includes the governor, who is the head of the executive branch, the lieutenant governor, the secretary of state, the attorney general, and the state treasurer. Among the jobs that the governor performs are the administration of state laws, the proposal of an agenda in the legislature, and the representation of the state in national and international settings. The governor is also chief of the armed forces in the state and may grant pardons for people convicted of crimes.

DID YOU KNOW?

In addition to national holidays, Colorado also officially celebrates the following three holidays: Susan B. Anthony Day (February 15), which honors a leader of the women's suffrage movement; Arbor Day (the third Friday in April), which raises environmental awareness; and Leif Ericson Day (October 9), which celebrates one of the first Europeans to reach North America.

Elected Posts in the Executive Branch

Office	Term	Term Limit
Governor	4 years	2 consecutive terms
Lieutenant Governor	4 years	2 consecutive terms
Secretary of State	4 years	2 consecutive terms
Attorney General	4 years	2 consecutive terms
Treasurer	4 years	2 consecutive terms

The office of the governor includes commissions on such issues as conservation, the arts, boxing, civil rights, and technology.

The attorney general is the chief lawyer for the state and head of the Department of Law. He or she prosecutes cases in the interest of the state and defends the state in court when claims are brought against it. The state treasurer has responsibility for seeing that tax revenues are well managed. The secretary of state is in charge of collecting information about the state and making this information available to the public. The secretary of state also oversees elections. Each of these officials is elected and serves a four-year term. Officers of the executive branch may hold their posts for only two terms in a row.

In 1966, Coloradans passed a constitutional amendment that changed the organization of the executive branch.

A Long Time Building

In 1868, Colorado businessman Henry Brown donated the land on which the Colorado capitol building now stands. It wasn't until 1890 that the building's cornerstone was laid. By November 1894, the governor and other government officers were able to conduct their business there, although the building was not yet completed. In 1908, the capitol's dome was leafed with Colorado gold, and the building was finally finished.

The amendment required the executive branch to consolidate its many agencies and boards into no more than twenty departments. These departments focus on issues such as education, health, safety, agriculture, and natural resources. The secretary of state, the attorney general, and the state treasurer each head one department. The remaining department heads are appointed by the governor and approved by the state senate.

Legislative Branch

In Colorado, the state legislature, where laws are proposed and passed, is called the General Assembly. The General Assembly is made up of a sixty-five member house of representatives and a thirty-five member senate. Senators serve for four years and representatives for two. Neither a representative nor a senator may serve for more than eight years in a row. The assembly passes bills that become laws and appropriations bills that fund state agencies. All bills are considered by committees before they are voted on. The assembly begins meeting on the second Wednesday in January each year. Sessions last for no more than 120 consecutive days, including weekends. Special sessions can be called by the governor or by a two-thirds vote of the assembly. Most legislators hold other jobs when the assembly is not in session. Only about 7 percent are full-time politicians. Nearly half are employed in business and industry, and slightly more than 10 percent are attorneys.

Judicial Branch

The judicial branch of Colorado's state government has four levels — the supreme court; appeals courts; district courts; and municipal, county, and police courts. The supreme court is the highest court in the state. Cases go to the supreme court only after they have been decided in other, lower courts. If there is a question about whether a verdict in one of the lower courts was properly reached, an appeal can be filed with the supreme court. The seven justices of the supreme

DID YOU KNOW?

Marble taken from quarries in Marble, Colorado, was used in the construction of the Lincoln Memorial, in Washington, D.C., and the Tomb of the Unknown Soldier, in Arlington, Virginia.

Colorado Leads the Way

On November 7, 1893, Colorado became the first state in the Union to approve women's suffrage in a popular election. Women gained the right to vote through an amendment to the state constitution that, in accordance with Colorado law, was passed by a majority vote of the state's citizens. Behind this radical action were women's organizations, labor unions, religious groups, and reform-minded people of every stripe — including Colorado's own governor, Davis H. Waite of Aspen. Women would not get the vote nationally until 1920.

General Assembly			
House	**Number of Members**	**Length of Term**	**Term Limits**
Senate	35 senators	4 years	2 consecutive terms
House of Representatives	65 representatives	2 years	4 consecutive terms

court decide whether to hear a case. To become a supreme court justice, a person must be proposed by a commission of ordinary citizens (not elected officials). The governor decides whether the proposed person will serve on the court. An appointed justice serves for two years and then must be elected by the public to remain in office. If the public approves, the justice then serves for ten more years. A justice may remain on the supreme court indefinitely, but he or she must be reelected every ten years by the voters.

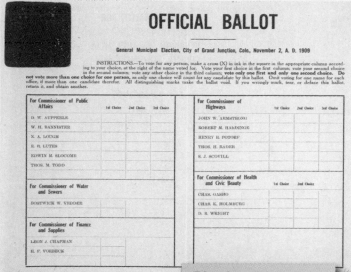

The court of appeals has sixteen judges who are appointed in the same way as supreme court justices but who serve eight-year terms. Below the appeals courts are the twenty-two district courts. Each district court has one or more judges, and these judges hear the major criminal and civil cases in the state. District court judges serve six-year terms but are appointed and elected just like supreme court and appellate court judges. Each of Colorado's sixty-three counties has its own court, and the largest of the more than 260 cities and towns have municipal courts.

National Government
Colorado elects two senators and six representatives to the U.S. Congress. Senators serve six-year terms, and representatives serve two-year terms. Measures to limit the terms of U.S. senators and representatives have been approved by Colorado voters but declared unconstitutional by the courts.

Local Government
In Colorado, a community with a population of two thousand or more may elect to have "home rule" and be governed by a charter. Home rule gives a community more control over its affairs than if it is governed directly by county government. Cities are governed by city councils, while towns are managed by boards of trustees. In Denver, the city and the county have exactly the same boundaries, so the area is governed by one set of officials, rather than two.

Playing Favorites
Colorado uses the preferential ballot. On this ballot, voters indicate whether a candidate is their first, second, or third choice. Any candidate who receives more than half of all the first-choice votes wins. If no one receives more than 50 percent, the least popular candidate is dropped from the ballot. Then, the votes of those people who listed the dropped candidate as their first choice are given to their second-choice candidates. The votes are then recounted. If there is still no clear winner, the least popular of the remaining candidates is dropped and the process continues until one candidate can be shown to have the clear majority of popular support.

The High Life

> Hundreds of persons are now permanent residents of Colorado, enjoying *perfect health,* who came here as a last resort in search of that inestimable boon.
>
> — Colorado, *a statement of facts prepared and published by the authority of the Territorial Board of Immigration, 1872*

Tourists flock to Colorado — and no wonder. The state has the kind of natural beauty that provides the basis for just about any outdoor sport. All the fun in Colorado isn't found outdoors, however. Towns and museums bring history to life, and cultural events of every variety are all set against the stunning backdrop of the Rocky Mountains.

▼ A daring skier takes on a vertical drop at Vail.

The Great Outdoors and More

Colorado skiing is among the best in the world. The wide-open slopes are covered with snow from late October through March and sometimes even April. During the winter, resort towns fill with skiers. Among Colorado's best-known ski resorts are Aspen, Vail, and Copper Mountain. Some resorts have been built in mining towns and retain some of the flavor of the Old West. These resort towns often become cultural centers during the summer. In Telluride, once a silver and gold mining town, summer visitors are treated to a variety of musical and theatrical festivals, including the Telluride Film Festival, a showcase for independent filmmakers. The entire town

of Telluride, with its picturesque Victorian houses, is a National Historic Landmark District. Some mountain towns, such as Ouray, feature hot springs where one can spend an afternoon relaxing in a natural hot tub while gazing up into the sky. Montrose, in the southwestern part of the state, is home to the Ute Indian Museum, which exhibits a collection of art and artifacts relating to the Ute people of the region. The museum also has a native plants garden on its grounds.

Ancient Culture and Natural Wonders

Southwestern Colorado is home to the remains of ancient civilizations. In Mesa Verde National Park, visitors can climb up to the houses that the Anasazi carved into the cliffs long before Europeans arrived in the area. Several complexes are maintained for people to explore, while others must be viewed from the valley below. Petroglyph Point, also within the park's boundaries, is a kind of outdoor gallery where the rock drawings of the Anasazi are permanently on display. The Cortez Cultural Center in nearby Cortez offers programs of Native-American dance, as well as poetry readings and tours of local archaeological sites.

Deep within the San Juan National Forest, also in southwestern Colorado, lies the Chimney Rock Archaeological Area. Two towers of freestanding rock give

Rocking the Rocks

The Red Rocks Amphitheatre, 15 miles (24 km) west of Denver, is a natural, open-air arena. Two massive rock formations, Ship Rock and Creation Rock, form the walls of the theater. Each rock is taller than Niagara Falls. The walls of Red Rocks are naturally decorated with the fossilized remains of dinosaurs and other prehistoric creatures. Businessman John Brisben Walker was the first to explore the possibilities of the area, once known as the Garden of Angels. He produced several concerts on the site between 1906 and 1910. In 1927, the Denver Parks Department bought the site for use as a public theater. Since Red Rocks opened in 1941, such internationally known artists as Igor Stravinsky, Benny Goodman, the Beatles, and U2 have performed in this majestic setting.

the area its name. At the top of a mesa are the remains of a settlement from one thousand years ago, including the foundations of an impressive kiva, which is a type of round shelter sunk into the rock and built up with careful stonework. This site may have been used by Native Americans to observe the stars, but no one knows for sure.

In the northwestern corner of the state, visitors will find the remains of dinosaurs that roamed the region more than 140 million years ago. Dinosaur National Monument has more than 200,000 acres (80,940 ha) of ruggedly beautiful scenery. The park's most interesting feature is Dinosaur Quarry, where the bones of many prehistoric beasts have been preserved in rocks. One of the best ways to see this park is to take a rafting trip through the deep chasms of the Green River.

City Life

Denver is a hot spot for cultural activity in Colorado. From Invesco Field at Mile High, where fans can follow the exploits of the city's National Football League (NFL) team,

▲ A hiker uses a log to traverse a stream in the Indian Peaks Wilderness Area. Located in the Arapaho and Roosevelt National Forests, this wilderness area covers 73,291 acres (29,661 ha) and includes remnants of ancient glaciers among its jagged peaks.

the Broncos, to the winding paths of its botanical gardens, Denver has plenty to offer visitors and residents alike. The theaters of the Denver Arts Complex provide a revolving menu of plays and other entertainment, while the city's lively downtown boasts more than one hundred restaurants and thirty art galleries.

Colorado Springs, to the south of Denver, offers spectacular views of Pikes Peak and is home to the U.S. Air Force Academy. There, men and women receive a college education and training in aviation skills such as navigation, parachuting, and flying, as well as combat skills.

Museums and Libraries

The Colorado History Museum in Denver celebrates the rich past of the state with dioramas and artifacts relating to Native American culture, Spanish exploration, and mining and ranching in the 1800s. The Black American West Museum and Heritage Center, also in Denver, explores the fascinating story of African Americans in the West. The Denver Art Museum houses a collection of more than forty thousand objects and has a particularly fine collection of Native American art. Reflecting the Denver area's importance as a mining center, there is an office of the U.S. Mint in Denver, where visitors may see how forty million coins are minted every day.

Other museums in the state celebrate Colorado's history. The Buffalo Bill Museum in Golden is dedicated to the legend of William Cody, known as Buffalo Bill. Cody was the founder of Buffalo Bill's Wild West Show, which toured the world in the nineteenth century. The show introduced audiences to the daredevil skills of western cowboys and the culture of western Native Americans. The Walsenburg Mining Museum features the culture of a nineteenth-century coal mining town. The museum is housed in an old jail.

▼ Paul Stewart, founder of the Black American West Museum and Heritage Center, stands near one of the museum's exhibits. Stewart has dedicated his museum to educating people about the contributions of African Americans to the development of the West, teaching visitors that one-third of all cowboys were black and that African Americans in the West filled every role, from barber to doctor to state legislator. African Americans were also among the West's first millionaires and fought heroically alongside Teddy Roosevelt in the Spanish-American War.

▶ Denver's Central
Library has more
than 4.5 million
items available
to the public.

The University of Colorado at Boulder is home to the CU Art Galleries. The galleries' Colorado Collection includes a variety of work, from American prints of the 1930s and 1940s to the works of the Old Masters.

The state's first public library opened in Denver in 1889. There are now 230 public libraries scattered throughout the state. The Colorado State Library in Denver collects written materials about Colorado history. The library system of the University of Colorado at Boulder has more than eleven million books, the largest collection of any one library in the Rocky Mountain region. In Denver, the Tattered Cover Bookstore, one of the largest and best-loved independent bookstores in the nation, offers four floors of browsing pleasure.

Communications

Colorado's first newspaper, the *Rocky Mountain News*, was published in 1859. Founded to serve the crowds of people arriving in the region in search of mining fortunes, the paper is still published daily. Together with the *Denver Post,* it is one of the state's two most popular papers. As of 2000, there were about 150 newspapers published in the state, about thirty of which were printed daily.

Sports

Colorado has five professional sports teams, all with home stadiums in Denver. The Colorado Avalanche, who play at Denver's Pepsi Center, is the state's National Hockey League (NHL) team. The Avalanche began playing in 1995

DID YOU KNOW?

The National Western Stock Show in Denver is the largest such event in the world. Thousands of cows, sheep, pigs, llamas, buffalo, and even yaks are brought to the show each year to be entered in competitions and sold to the highest bidders. The show began in 1906. A horse show was added in 1907 and a rodeo in 1932. In 2000, more than 630,000 people attended the event.

Sport	Team	Home
Baseball	Colorado Rockies	Coors Field, Denver
Basketball	Denver Nuggets	Pepsi Center, Denver
Football	Denver Broncos	Invesco Field at Mile High, Denver
Hockey	Colorado Avalanche	Pepsi Center, Denver
Soccer	Colorado Rapids	Invesco Field at Mile High, Denver

and won the Stanley Cup that same season and again in 2001. The Denver Nuggets, who share the Pepsi Center with the Avalanche, are the state's National Basketball Association (NBA) team. They began life as the Denver Rockets in the American Basketball Association (ABA) but became the Nuggets in 1974 and joined the NBA in 1976. The team is named for the little chunks of gold that brought so many people to the state in the nineteenth century.

The Colorado Rockies play at Coors Field. One of Major League Baseball's newest teams, the Rockies began playing in 1993.

The Colorado Rapids is the state's professional soccer team. The team has been playing since 1996 and can be seen at Invesco Field at Mile High. The Rapids share the stadium with Colorado's National Football League team, the Denver Broncos. The Broncos are perhaps best known for one player — John Elway. An outstanding quarterback, Elway was a Bronco for sixteen years. In 1998, he led his team to victory in Super Bowl XXXII. The Broncos won again the next year and Elway retired as a champion.

▼ Denver Bronco star running back Terrell Davis plows through the defensive line.

Colorful Coloradans

There are women so shrewd as to manage to make a husband support them. There are others smart enough to take care of themselves and husbands too.

— Caroline Churchill in the Queen Bee, *Denver's first women's rights newspaper, July 5, 1892*

Following are only a few of the thousands of people who were born, died, or spent much of their lives in Colorado and made extraordinary contributions to the state and the nation.

BARNEY FORD
CIVIL RIGHTS ADVOCATE

BORN: *circa 1822, Virginia*
DIED: *circa 1902, Denver*

Born into slavery, Barney Launcelot Ford escaped to Chicago, later helping other slaves to freedom. After moving to Nicaragua and running two successful hotels, he returned to Chicago and opened a stable, which also served as a stop on the Underground Railroad. In 1860, Ford and his family moved to Colorado. His attempts to stake a mining claim were thwarted by white men who drove him off his claim. Ford settled in Denver, where he became a successful hotel owner. His lavish hotels in Denver and Cheyenne were among the best in the West. Ford continued to offer support to escaped slaves and started the first adult education classes for African Americans in Colorado. He lobbied successfully against the first proposed constitution for the state because he did not feel that it protected African-American civil rights. After Colorado became a state, Ford was the first African American to serve on a Colorado grand jury.

HELEN HUNT JACKSON
AUTHOR

BORN: *October 15, 1830, Amherst, MA*
DIED: *August 12, 1885, San Francisco, CA*

Helen Maria Fiske became a successful author of children's stories, novels, and poetry after the death of her first husband, Edward Hunt, in 1863. She suffered from poor health, and a doctor recommended a change of climate. In 1875, she traveled to Colorado, where she met and married William Jackson of Colorado Springs. While visiting the East Coast, she attended a lecture that made her aware of the struggles of Native Americans. Jackson took up the cause of Native American rights and wrote several books that drew national attention. Most notable among her works was *Century of Dishonor* (1881). Later, Jackson was appointed a special commissioner to investigate the living conditions of Native Americans who lived on Catholic missions in California.

CHIEF OURAY
UTE LEADER
BORN: *circa 1833, near Taos, NM*
DIED: *August 24, 1880, Ignacio*

Chief Ouray, whose name means "the Arrow," was the leader of the Uncompahgre band in the Ute nation. As the Ute's diplomat, he met with President Ulysses S. Grant in 1868 and turned over some Ute land, including territory in the San Juan Mountains, hoping to stop settlers from seizing more. U.S. settlers ignored this agreement and began mining on Ute land. In 1879, a group of Ute killed Nathan Meeker, a federal employee who had tried to force the Ute to adopt the settlers' culture. His staff was killed and several women were taken hostage. Ouray negotiated the release of the hostages. U.S. president Rutherford Hayes admired Ouray's skills as a negotiator and called him "the most intelligent man I've ever conversed with."

WILLIAM HENRY JACKSON
PHOTOGRAPHER
BORN: *April 4, 1843, Keesville, NY*
DIED: *June 30, 1942, New York, NY*

William Henry Jackson began taking pictures at age twelve. In 1870, he was hired by the U.S. Geological Survey to photograph the West. Jackson was the first person to photograph what would later become Yellowstone National Park. Jackson's photographs so impressed members of the U.S. Congress that they designated Yellowstone as the world's first national park in 1872. After traveling throughout the West and taking pictures of ancient cliff dwellings in Colorado, Jackson settled in Denver and opened a photography studio. His portrayal of the majesty of the West's natural landscape helped stir interest in the region and made him Colorado's most famous photographer.

THE UNSINKABLE MOLLY BROWN
SUFFRAGIST
BORN: *July 18, 1867, Hannibal, MO*
DIED: *October 26, 1932, New York, NY*

When she was eighteen, Margaret Tobin moved to Leadville, where she met and married James Joseph Brown. Soon after their marriage in 1886, Brown's husband struck it rich. In 1894, they moved to Denver, where Margaret Brown helped organize the Denver Women's Club and the Colorado chapter of the American Women's Suffrage Association. In 1909, the Browns separated. Known as Maggie (never Molly) Brown, she began traveling the world. In 1912, she became famous as a survivor of the wreck of the ocean liner *Titanic*. Brown helped organize passengers on the sinking ship and loaded five lifeboats before she was forced to board the sixth. Newspapers began to call her Unsinkable Molly Brown and to publish tall tales about her life. Brown used her fame to draw attention to international issues. She organized the International Women's Rights conference that was held in Newport, Rhode Island in 1914.

BENJAMIN B. LINDSEY
JUDGE

BORN: *November 25, 1869, Jackson, TN*
DIED: *March 26, 1943, Los Angeles, CA*

Benjamin Barr Lindsey was a judge and reformer. He changed the way young people who have committed crimes are treated. Lindsey founded and presided over the juvenile court in Denver from 1900 to 1927. He and other reformers believed young people who had committed crimes should not be sentenced in the same way as adults, and that juvenile offenders should not serve their sentences in prisons with adults. Lindsey was also an advocate for liberalizing divorce laws and an outspoken enemy of the Ku Klux Klan.

FLORENCE RENA SABIN
SCIENTIST

BORN: *November 9, 1871, Central City*
DIED: *October 3, 1953, Denver*

In 1896, Florence Rena Sabin entered the Johns Hopkins University Medical School in Baltimore, Maryland. As a student, she created a model of an infant's brain stem, which was later widely used in medical schools. In 1917, she became the first woman appointed to a full professorship at Johns Hopkins Medical School. A brilliant researcher, Sabin was the first woman to be elected president of the American Association of Anatomists, in 1924. In 1925, she made history again, twice, by becoming the first woman elected to the National Academy of Sciences and the first woman invited to join the Rockefeller Institute of Medical Research. After retiring, Sabin moved to Denver, where she reorganized the state's health department. In 1948, Sabin became head of the Denver Department of Health.

HATTIE McDANIEL
ACTOR

BORN: *June 10, 1895, Wichita, KS*
DIED: *October 26, 1952, Hollywood, CA*

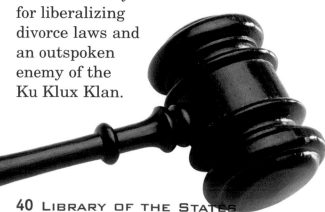

The daughter of a former slave, Hattie McDaniel moved to Fort Collins when she was five years old. When she was thirteen, she began performing in local minstrel shows, which both celebrated and stereotyped African-American culture for white audiences. After early success, McDaniel's career took a downturn, and she worked as a cook and washerwoman. She once joked that she "washed three million dishes on [her] way to stardom." McDaniel eventually moved to Hollywood and began to get regular work in movies. In 1939, McDaniel landed the role of Mammy in *Gone with the Wind*. McDaniel, together with advisers from the National Association for the Advancement of Colored People (NAACP), successfully urged the movie's director, David Selznick, to remove some of the script's racist language. McDaniel won an Oscar for her portrayal of Mammy, becoming the first African American to win the award.

JACK DEMPSEY
BOXER

BORN: *June 24, 1895, Manassa*
DIED: *May 31, 1983, New York, NY*

William Harrison Dempsey began his professional boxing career at the age of nineteen. After delivering a series of notable knockouts, he became known as "the Manassa Mauler." The majority of his knockouts came in the first round. Dempsey held the world heavyweight boxing champion title from 1919 to 1926. A famous 1924 painting by George Bellows depicts Dempsey's 1923 defeat of Argentine boxer Luis Firpo. In a career of eighty-four fights, lasting from 1914 to 1940, he won sixty-two, knocking out his opponent in fifty-one bouts. After retiring from boxing, Dempsey served as a lieutenant commander in the U.S. Coast Guard during World War II and later became a successful restaurant owner in New York City.

SCOTT CARPENTER
ASTRONAUT

BORN: *May 1, 1925, Boulder*

Malcolm Scott Carpenter grew up in the high altitudes of Boulder and attended the University of Colorado, earning a degree in aeronautical engineering in 1949. That same year he was commissioned in the U.S. Navy. He flew a variety of dangerous missions during the Korean War, from 1951 to 1953. In 1959, Carpenter was selected as one of seven astronauts on the Mercury Project, which sent the first U.S. astronauts into space. Carpenter was the second U.S. man to orbit Earth, traveling around the planet three times on May 24, 1962. In later life, Carpenter turned to deep-sea exploration, adding the title of aquanaut to that of astronaut. Carpenter remains an active member of the Explorer's Club, an association of space explorers.

FIFTEEN CENTS

TIME
The Weekly News-Magazine

VOL. II NO. 2   CHAMPION DEMPSEY
*"The solution of an ancient problem"—
see page 14*   SEPT. 10, 1923

Colorado

History At-A-Glance

1682
René-Robert Cavelier, Sieur de La Salle, claims the Louisiana territory, including part of Colorado, for France.

1706
Juan de Ulibarri and his soldiers arrive in Colorado and claim it for Spain.

1803
Part of present-day Colorado is included in the Louisiana Purchase.

1806
Zebulon Pike explores Colorado, and sees, but does not climb, the peak that will be named after him.

1820
Stephen Long leads an expedition through the Colorado region.

1848
United States given control of southern Colorado through Treaty of Guadalupe-Hidalgo, which ends the Mexican War.

1851
First permanent U.S. settlement in Colorado established at San Luis.

1858
William Russell discovers gold near Denver. Discovery leads to Colorado gold rush.

1861
U.S. Congress creates Colorado Territory.

1862
Oil is discovered in Colorado, near Florence.

1864
Third Colorado Cavalry attacks sleeping Arapaho and Cheyenne at Sand Creek, killing several hundred men, women, and children.

1876
Colorado wins statehood.

1600   **1700**   **1800**

1492
Christopher Columbus comes to New World.

1607
Capt. John Smith and three ships land on Virginia coast and start first English settlement in New World — Jamestown.

1754–63
French and Indian War.

1773
Boston Tea Party.

1776
Declaration of Independence adopted July 4.

1777
Articles of Confederation adopted by Continental Congress.

1787
U.S. Constitution written.

1812–14
War of 1812.

United States

History At-A-Glance

CRAIG HIGH SCHOOL FOOT-BALL TEAM.

1879
Nathan Meeker, government representative to Ute reservation, is killed in uprising.

1893
Sherman Silver Purchase Act repealed, drastically lowering the price of silver.

1893
Colorado women win the right to vote in all state elections.

1896
William Jennings Bryan makes "Cross of Gold" speech.

1908
Colorado's state capitol building in Denver is completed.

1914
Striking coal miners and family members die in the Ludlow Massacre.

1934
Gold Reserve Act helps Colorado silver industry.

1958
U.S. Air Force Academy opens at Colorado Springs.

1963
First liver transplant performed at University of Colorado Health Sciences Center.

1968
Colorado River Basin Development Act becomes law. Act helps to redistribute water throughout state.

1973
Eisenhower Tunnel is built under the Continental Divide.

1998
Denver Broncos win their first Super Bowl.

1800	1900	2000

1848
Gold discovered in California draws eighty thousand prospectors in the 1849 Gold Rush.

1861–65
Civil War.

1869
Transcontinental railroad completed.

1917–18
U.S. involvement in World War I.

1929
Stock market crash ushers in Great Depression.

1941–45
U.S. involvement in World War II.

1950–53
U.S. fights in the Korean War.

1964–73
U.S. involvement in Vietnam War.

2000
George W. Bush wins the closest presidential election in history.

2001
A terrorist attack in which four hijacked airliners crash into New York City's World Trade Center, the Pentagon, and farmland in western Pennsylvania leaves thousands dead or injured.

▼ **Football teams and basketball teams from Meeker and Craig High Schools at Craig circa 1920.**

MEEKER-HIGH-SCHOOL-FOOT-BALL-TEAM

Festivals and Fun for All

Check web site for exact date and directions.

Carbondale Mountain Fair, Carbondale

This summer festival in the mountain town of Carbondale offers an abundance of local arts, crafts, and cultural events.
www.carbondale.com/ccah

Chile & Frijole Festival, Pueblo

Each September, Pueblo invites people to share its celebration of locally grown hot peppers and food that reflects the region's Mexican heritage.
www.pedco.org/community

Colorado State Fair, Pueblo

From mid-August to early September, the biggest and best of Colorado agriculture, livestock, and home crafts are on display at this lively celebration of the state.
www.coloradostatefair.com

Four Corners Folk Festival, Pagosa Springs

This end-of-the-summer festival showcases folk music from around the United States.
www.folkwest.com

Four Corners Monument, Four Corners

Stand, sit, or lie in Utah, Colorado, New Mexico, and Arizona simultaneously. Who says you can't be four places at once?
www.navajonationparks.org

....

▶ Greeley's Independence Stampede features steer roping.

Ghost Walk Through Pioneer Cemetery, Glenwood Springs

This annual event in late October features visits to the graves of famous pioneers, such as Doc Holliday, and storytelling about the town's Wild West days.
www.glenwoodsprings.net

Greeley Independence Stampede, Greeley

The Greeley Stampede is the nation's largest Fourth of July rodeo festival, featuring a parade and country dancing, as well as a wide variety of rodeo competitions.
www.greeleystampede.org

International Buskerfest, Denver

During the last weekend in June, Denver streets are filled with outdoor performers, known as buskers. Magicians, acrobats, puppeteers, and other artists astonish visitors.
www.buskerfest.com

International Snow Sculpture Competition, Breckenridge

Since 1991, the Breckenridge Ski Resort has been producing artificially-made

▶ Molly Brown's Denver home.

snow for use in the construction of snow sculptures in this international competition. The sculptures, which are designed and built by four-person teams with only hand tools, can weigh up to 20 tons.
www.gobreckevents.com

The Meeker Classic Sheepdog Championship Trials, Meeker

Good dogs prove their worth in this five-day event in September. Sheepdogs compete in a number of events. A dog agility contest and a border collie Frisbee exhibition also are featured.
www.meekersheepdog.com

Molly Brown House Museum, Denver

Visit the house where the "Unsinkable Molly Brown," famous survivor of the *Titanic* disaster and advocate of women's rights, lived when she was not traveling the world.
www.mollybrown.org

Mountain Dew Vertical Challenge

Skiers of all ages and abilities compete amidst breathtaking scenery at Colorado's top resorts.
www.mountaindewverticalchallenge.com

Rocky Mountain Balloon Festival, Denver

Come to the highest state in the nation to watch brave balloonists travel even farther into the sky. This two-day event in August offers exhibitions of balloon flight, lighted balloons at night, and a jazz festival.
www.rockymountainballoonfestival.com

Telluride Film Festival, Telluride

Although the natural splendor of Telluride is breathtaking, visitors come to this spot annually to spend hours in dark rooms watching movies. Since 1974, this festival has been showcasing some of the most original independent and foreign films.
www.telluridefilmfestival.com

Vail Arts Festival, Vail

Every June, this picturesque former mining town, now a mecca for skiers, presents a competitive arts festival in which one hundred artists are chosen to present their work to the public.
www.vailartsfestival.com

Books

Collier, Grant. *Colorado: Yesterday and Today*. Montrose, CO: Western Reflections Publishing, 2001. Called "one of the best books of 2001" by the *Rocky Mountain News*, this collaboration by Grant Collier and his great-great-grandfather tells the story of Colorado in photographs.

Downey, Matthew. *Colorado: Crossroads of the West*. Boulder, CO: Pruett Publishing Co., 1998. Look back at Colorado's colorful history.

Goodman, Susan. *Stones, Bones, and Petroglyphs: Digging into Southwest Archaeology*. New York, NY: Simon & Schuster, 1998. Learn more about how archaeologists uncover the stories hidden in rocks and earth.

Iversen, Kristen. *Molly Brown: Unraveling the Myth*. Boulder, CO: Johnson Books, 1999. Read about the adventurous life of Margaret "Unsinkable Molly" Brown.

Krudwig, Vickie Leigh. *Hiking Through Colorado History*. Englewood, CO: Westcliffe Publishing, 1998. Go on adventures in Colorado while learning about the state's history, from the formation of the Rocky Mountains to twentieth-century life.

Web Sites

▶ Official Colorado state web site
www.colorado.gov

▶ Official web site of Denver, Colorado's capital
www.denvergov.org

▶ Official web site of the Colorado Historical Society
www.coloradohistory.org

▶ Official web site of the Colorado Tourism Office
www.colorado.com

Note: Page numbers in *italics* refer to maps, illustrations, or photographs.

A

Adams, Alva, 14
African Americans, 13, 18, 35, 40–41
age distribution, 16
agriculture, 10, 11, *12,* 24, 26
Air Force Academy, 19, 35
airports, 27
altitude, 7
Anasazi Indians, 4, 8, 9, 33
animals, 6, *21,* 23
Arapaho Indians, 8
Arbor Day, 28
architecture, 29, 32–33
area, 6
Arikaree River, 20
Arkansas River, 21, 22
arts, 32–33, 40–41
Aspen, Colorado, 15, 32
attractions, 7, 44–45
Auraria, Colorado, 19
Aurora, Colorado, 6

B

baseball, 26, *26,* 37
basketball, 37
Bates, Katherine Lee, 7
Battle of Ludlow, 4
beer brewing, 26
bighorn sheep, 6
bird (state), 6
Bishop's Castle, 7
Black American West Museum and Heritage Center, 35, *35*
Boulder, Colorado, 19
Brown, Clara, 13
Brown, Henry, 29
Brown, Margaret Tobin (Molly), 39–40
Bryan, William Jennings, 13
Buffalo Bill Museum, 35

C

capital, 6
capitol building, 29, *29*
Carbondale Mountain Fair, 44
Carpenter, Scott, 41
Cavelier, René-Robert (Sieur de La Salle), 8
Central City, Colorado, 13
Central Library, *36*
Century of Dishonor (Jackson), 39
Charles, Ray, 7
Cheyenne Indians, 8
Chief Ouray, 39, *39*
Chile & Frijole Festival, 44
Chimney Rock Archaeological Area, 33

Chivington, John, 11
Churchill, Caroline, 38
cities, *5,* 6, 34–35. *See also specific cities*
Civil War, 10–11
Cliff Dwellers, 4, 8, *9,* 33
climate, 21, 23
coal, 26
Cody, William (Buffalo Bill), 35
Colorado History Museum, 35
Colorado Plateau, 20, 21
Colorado River, 9, 21
Colorado Rockies, 26
Colorado Springs, Colorado, 6, 19, 23, 35
Colorado State Fair, 44
Colorado State Library, 36
Comanche Indians, 8
commerce, 24–27
communications, 36–37
constitution, 28, 29
Continental Divide, 4, 20
Coors Field, *26,* 37
Copper Mountain, Colorado, 32
Cortez Cultural Center, 33
courts, 30–31
Craig, Colorado, 14
Creation Rock, *33*
Cripple Creek, 14
CU Art Galleries, 36
culture, 32–37

D

Davis, Terrell, *37*
Dempsey, Jack, 4, 41, *41*
Denver, Colorado, 6, 10, *10, 18,* 19, 21, 35, *36*
Denver, James, 10
Denver, John, 16
Denver Arts Complex, 35
Denver Broncos, 37
Denver International Airport, *27*
Denver Parks Department, 33
Denver Post, 36
Dinosaur National Monument, 34
Doc Holliday, 44
Dole, Charles, 15
drought, 14
Durango, Colorado, 20
"Durango Mountain Caballero" (Denver), 16

E

Echo Lake, *20*
economy and commerce
agriculture, 10, 11, *12,* 24, 26
Great Depression and recovery, 14–15
gross state product, *25*
manufacturing, 15, 24, 25–26

mining, 4, 12–15, 24, 26, 36
standard of living, 19
tourism, 15, 24, 27, 32
transportation, *5,* 27
education, 18, 19
Edwin C. Johnson Memorial Tunnel, 27
Eisenhower Memorial Tunnel, 27
elected offices, 29
Elway, John, 4, 37
employers, 24
environmental issues, 15
ethnic makeup of Colorado, 17–18
events, 7, 44–45
executive branch, 28–30
explorers, 8, 33

F

famous persons, 38–41
Ferris, Warren Angus, 8
festivals, 44–45
fish (state), 6
fishing, 23
flower (state), 6
food processing, 26
football, 34–35, 37, *37*
Ford, Barney, 38
forests, 22
Fort Collins, Colorado, 6, 14
fossil (state), 6
Four Corners Folk Festival, 44
Four Corners Monument, 44
Four Corners region, 20
Front Range, 21
fur trade, 9

G

Garden of Angels, 33
Garden of the Gods, *23*
gemstone (state), 6
General Assembly, 30
geography, 20–23
Georgetown, Colorado, 12
glaciers, 21
gold, 4, 10, 14
Gold Reserve Act, 14
Golden, Colorado, *19,* 26
Gone With the Wind (film), 41
governmental structure, 28–31. *See also* politics and political figures
Grand Lake, 21
Grand Mesa National Forest, 7
Grant, Ulysses S., 39
Great Depression, 14–15
Great Plains, 20, 21
Greeley, Horace, *11,* 11
Greeley Independence Stampede, *44*
Green River, 34

gross state product, *25*
Gunnison National Forest, *4–5*

H

Hayes, Rutherford, 39
highways, *5*
Hispanic population, 18
history of Colorado, 8–15, *42–43*
hockey, 15, 36-37
home rule, 31
house of representatives, 30

I

immigration, 16
income, 19
Indian Peaks Wilderness Area, *34*
initiatives, 28
insect (state), 6
International Buskerfest, 44
International Snow Sculpture Competition, 44–45
Invesco Field at Mile High, 34, 37

J

Jackson, Helen Hunt, 38–39, *38*
Jackson, William Henry, 4, 39
Jefferson, Thomas, 9
judicial branch, 30–31

K

Kit Carson County Carousel, 7
kivas, 34

L

La Salle, René-Robert Cavelier, Sieur de, 8
Lake Granby, 21
lakes, 21–22, 23
Lakewood, Colorado, 6
Lamm, Richard, 28
Leadville, Colorado, 13
Legal Tender Act, 14
legislative branch, 30
Leif Ericson Day, 28
libraries, 35
lifestyle, 32–37
Lincoln Memorial, 30
Lindsey, Benjamin B., 40
literature, 38–39
local government, 31
Long, Stephen, 9
Louis XIV, 8
Louisiana Purchase, 9
Loveland, Colorado, 7
Ludlow, Colorado, 13, *13*
lumber industry, 22

M

Mallen, Caroline, 12
manufacturing, 15, 24, 25–26

maps of Colorado, 5, *22,* 25
marble, 30
Maroon Bells-Snowmass
    Wilderness, *4–5*
Maroon Lake, *4–5*
McDaniel, Hattie, 41
McDonald, Jesse, 14
McKinley, William, 13
Meeker, Nathan C., 11, 12, 39
The Meeker Classic
    Sheepdog Championship
    Trials, 45
Mesa Verde National
    Park, *9,* 33
mesas, 7
Miller, Glenn, 4
mining, 4, 12–15, 24, 26, 36
Moffat Tunnel, 27
Molly Brown House
    Museum, 45
Montrose, Colorado, 33
motto (state), 6
Mount Elbert, 12, *20,* 20, 21
Mountain Dew Vertical
    Challenge, 45
museums, 35, 45
music, 33

N
national government, 31
National Western Stock
    Show, 36
Native Americans, 8–9,
    10–11, 34, 35, 39
New Deal, 14
newspapers, 36–37
nickname of Colorado, 11

O
oil, *14,* 26
outdoor recreation, 32–33, 34

P
Park Range, 21
Parker, Henry, 18
parks, 7, *9,* 18, 21, 23, 33
Peabody, James, 14
Perkins, Charles, 23
Petroglyph Point, 33

Pike, Zebulon, 9
Pikes Peak, 7, 20, 21, 35
pioneers, 4
plants, 22
politics and political figures
    Adams, Alva, 14
    Chief Ouray, 39, *39*
    governmental structure,
        28–31
    Grant, Ulysses S., 39
    Hayes, Rutherford, 39
    Jefferson, Thomas, 9
    Lindsey, Benjamin B., 40
    Louis XIV, 8
    McDonald, Jesse, 14
    Peabody, James, 14
    Populist party, 13
    Roosevelt, Franklin D.,
        14, 15
population, 6, 12, 15, 16–19
Populist party, 13
preferential ballot, *31*
public lands, 18–19
Pueblo Indians, 8

R
racial makeup of
    Colorado, 17–18
radio, 7
railroads, 7, *20,* 27
rainfall, 21, 23
ranching, 12, *24*
range wars, 12
Red Rocks Amphitheatre, *33*
Red Rocks Park, 7
religion, 19
Reorganization Act, 14
Rio Grande River, 21
rivers, 4, *5,* 20, 21–22, 23
roads, *5*
Rockefeller, John D., 13
Rocky Mountain Balloon
    Festival, 45
Rocky Mountain News, 36
Rocky Mountains, 4, 20,
    21, 27
rodeos, *44*
Roosevelt, Franklin D., 14, 15
Royal Gorge, 22

Russell, William, 10
Ruxton, George Frederick, 20

S
Sabin, Florence Rena, 4, 40
San Juan Mountains, 21
San Juan National Forest, 33
San Luis, Colorado, 10
Sand Creek Massacre, 11
Sangre de Cristo
    Mountains, 21
Sawatch Range, 21
schools, *19*
seal of Colorado, *28*
senate, 30
settlers, 4, 9–10
Sherman Silver Purchase
    Act, 13
Ship Rock, *33*
silver, 4, 12, 13
skiing, *15, 32,* 32, 45
snowfall, 21, 23
soccer, 37
song (state), 6
South Platte River, 21
Southern Ute, 11
Spain, 9-10, 18
Spiritualism, 12
sports, 26, 37, 41, *42–43*
standard of living, 19
statehood, 6, 11–13
Stewart, Paul, *35*
strikes, 13
Susan B. Anthony Day, 28

T
Tattered Cover Bookstore, 36
Telluride, Colorado, 32–33
Telluride Film Festival, 32, 45
temperature, 21, 23
Tenth Mountain Division, 15
Thompson, Mabel, 7
Thompson, Ted, 7
time line of Colorado
    history, *42–43*
Tomb of the Unknown
    Soldier, 30
tourism, 15, 24, 27, 32
trains, 7, 20, 27

transportation, 5, 27
tree (state), 6
trees, *20, 22*
Trinidad, Colorado, 4

U
Ulibarri, Juan de, 9
Union Colony, Colorado, 11
unions, 13
United Mine Workers of
    America, 13
University of Colorado, 19
uranium, 15
urbanization, 16
U.S. Mint, 35
Ute Indians, 8–9, 11, 12, 16,
    17, 39, *39*
Ute Indian Museum, 33

V
Vail, Colorado, *15, 32*
Vail Arts Festival, 45
Valentine's Day cards, 7
Victor, Colorado, 10
voting, 14, 31

W
Walker, John Brisben, 33
Walsenburg Mining Museum,
    36
Ward, Samuel, 7
waterfalls, 21
waterways, *5. See also* rivers
Wheat Ridge, *12*
White River National Forest,
    4–5
wildflowers, 22
wildlife, 6, *21,* 23
Womack, Robert, 14
women of Colorado, 4, 7, 12,
    13, 38–41
World War I, 14
World War II, 15

Y
Yellowstone National Park, 39